THE DAY THE PERFECT SPEAKERS LEFT

The Day

The Perfect Speakers

Left

By LEONARD NATHAN

Wesleyan University Press

MIDDLETOWN, CONNECTICUT

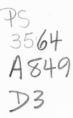

Some of these poems have previously appeared elsewhere. For their courtesy in granting permission to reprint and in assigning copyrights, grateful acknowledgment is made to the editors of the following:

Antioch Review; Epoch; Kenyon Review; Minnesota Review; New Republic; New York Times; Northwest Review; Perspective; Prairie Schooner; Quarterly Review of Literature; Quire; Shenandoah; UCLAN Review; A Western Sampler (Talisman Press); and The Performing Voice in Literature (Little, Brown and Company).

"Of Those Who Only Waited," "The Sacrifice" (originally titled "You Think It's Going to Be Easy") "The Summons" (originally titled "No Interpretations, Please"), and "Word from Your Victim" first appeared in the Massachusetts Review.

"Annunciation," "I Would Write More," "Nightwatch" (originally titled "Remember to Close the Door as You Go Out"), "Translating an Ancient Fragment," and "Translation from the Wind of Guadalajara" first appeared in Poetry.

Library of Congress Catalog Card Number: 69-17791
Manufactured in the United States of America
FIRST EDITION

For VERNON PATTERSON

Contents

THE DAY THE PERFECT SPEAKERS LEFT

Here are three hundred thousand doors,
Not counting the iron grates of cells,
The brassy portals of institutions,
Or the red upholstered gates of bars.

You want so much to be at home,
To arrive at the absolute address
Which richly keeps for you alone —
The right man in the right room.

She has everything ready and now waits,
But here are three hundred thousand doors;
They can drink you to death. The grayest hotels
Seem honeycombs these rainy nights.

Sometime you'll tarry. Behind one lock
A delicate music sings for you,
Or is that all in your head? The doors
On either side watch as you knock.

There are voices in water going steadily down the drain.
My God, am I throwing away some saving message?
You've heard that talk babbling below the wash.

Or a heater hissing in the corner of the empty basement:
What hurried whispering just under its steadiness
Goes up the chimney as inarticulate vapor?

You say there are no voices in wind, under water,
No speech in things that another human has not,
By force, put there. Then what is this urgent garble,

Like the flutter of girls to the tune of a swift little stream?
And it all runs into the sea or lapses to air.
When there's nothing else, I even listen to silence.

Whose cry was it that came through the fur of sleep?
I was dreaming of long rain and last fall dissolving.
And this wife in my arms, and this warm bed most real;
Then whose cry was it?

The rain, blowing across the open back windows,
Went down to dissolve the stunned grass, dissolve
The earth, and the lawn chairs rattled in the wind.
Clanked with the cold spatter.

But whose was the cry? This much, a woman's voice,
A call repeated high up the wind through rain,
Saying, "King of the rain, come out, come out,"
Over and over saying that.

I held on tighter each cry and, sweating the answer,
Thought: "The truth is I'm getting on in years;
Haven't been well of late, and here is this wife
Helpless in her own dream."

Still, "King of the rain, come out"; no mercy
But this one chance to find the voice in rain —
A queen's voice, commanding? And the chairs rattled,
Harangued by the hard drops.

It was July and one dog barked in the whole world
And dawn was bone dry and the lawn chairs were still;
But here was this wife, this bed, that dream, myself
In a sweat of sick waking.

What cry, you ask? The back windows were closed and curtained,
And what king of the rain I was not? And who is this wife
Sleeping in the peril of her own dream? My mood
Is not the mood of the weather.

You know how the boys next morning talk: they say
They've had exquisite virgins by the gross
And drunk the center of the city dry.
They wink and write their bragging off to loss.

Maybe a single bare bulb overhead
Has fouled their fantasies with dirty light;
Or maybe the bony girl they coldly had
Required a dry bed for one rainy night.

We've felt that idiot pang, come dawn, and pulled
The covers to our chins. The truth of it
Sounds in the coughing of a petty cold
Contracted in the bottom of some pit.

By noon, of course, the world was gold unspent,
And young, with nothing yet quite real to do,
We made a kind of sorry testament,
Lying for beauty better than we knew.

Come to shake me like the dripping midnight messenger,
Ghost of disaster — the thought of you suddenly
At the foot of my bed with the all-canceling truth!
"Say it, say it, dear heart!"

But you shook your head like one who knows she's about
To disappoint the third redeeming wish,
And said in a flat voice,"Nothing has changed,"
And darkened into your background.

Why, I had imagined transactions in Hell to get
You here, the rasp of transgressing spades in the night,
God knows what spells to lay you to rest again,
And for what? "Nothing has changed."

So the silence filled up with rain and it was hours back
To sleep where white iris, as far as dreaming could see,
Attended the shifty wind as a kind of distraction
From waiting, and you not there.

THE MODEL

I don't want to remember you in the furry hood
Under the snowing pines of Vaux, or strolling deeply
In the scarlet cannas of Tor Gardens, a sun hat
Tied on with a ribbon, one hand shading your eyes,
The other half-lifted to wave, or gowned for the great party
At Samson's, or at Clive Beach, oiled shoulders nude,
Hair knotted, a cloud of bronze, and the sun leaping back
Like a pang from your amber glasses.
                                    But that small dry voice
In the dark, tearing the pictures up, as if your body
Were the fast sister who got all the boys, you who have never
Trusted your father and take beauty to work
Like a skill from night school: this I'd remember, but cannot.

To make a goddess from fragments of polished marble,
Suns from reflections shadowed on the sea —

Your profile suddenly there, interposed between
The black curtain of midnight and me.

Candle, a stagy illumination; music,
A cheap accord; and this foolish wine...

A lion looks up from a deer, his eyes rounding
On many hidden things, as mine.

These eyes, a marble profile, a cold light
On gray water—parts of that whole?

I'm a different simpler man. O, candle, music,
This cloudy wine! — my hairs crawl.

I don't care what you think, beloved! I don't
Even care who you are. All that doesn't matter.
There is a fox in your purse or in your heart.

It is she I am really after, your hidden namesake,
A little beauty, tawny but well concealed,
Like a shadow of sex before the lights go out.

But not sex, not quite that, a way of arriving
Before or after that. It is in such instances
That the enduring lovers have met their match and whooped.

Put this in a book, beloved, and give the book
To old men, or fill out a form and sign it
With any of your aliases: It is the fox that survives.

You say I am unfeeling, that you are more than that. No.
I feel what I see. You are a little beauty,
You are that part of yourself that you will let loose

At the right instant. I didn't invent this world.
Ask Juan, ask Helen, ask the fox, ask your mother.
Yes, we can be friends; of course, we can be friends.

Fleets sank, horses went up in smoke,
When you curved around the corner
Of the building, leaving the world flat.

Two dimensions are left. The other
Has run off with a salesman from Cockayne
Where they sip their amber dew from goblets.

This is a book of cut-outs. I'm waiting
To be cut out, stood up, then blown over
By the first wind bearing your scent.

Straight talk misses you. So I've bent it.

APOLOGY

Woman may be the "temptation to finitude" as Kirkegaard thought when he
sacrificed his fiancee, Regina Olson, to
God, but the road to God is through
"fulfilled finitude."
> — Maurice Friedman

Even if you are not the road to God,
Regina, I would be tempted by your finitude,
Your — as I see it — gust of lucid hair,
Your blurred mouth, through the lucid hair, that asks
In tones as clear as Nordic air, "But why?"
Silence. What do these theologians know,
Their black cloaks flapping in the godless wind?
Their smoky glasses misbelieve, as you,
Your white dress tightened by the longing wind,
Light them the contour of a woman's form.
What on earth should God have made but this!
To Hell with them, Regina. So, one turns
His back, twitches his black cloak round him tight,
And loses heaven the instant that you drop
Your eyes — one hand extended, open, pale.
My hand, Regina. Nothing has been disclosed.
Love has not shown a glimmer of his grace
As yet. Say yes, Regina, yes, and all
The finitudes will sing how good to be,
Saved by the blessing body of your word.

I'm hurrying through this fog, but know where I'm going.
I can hear the sea to my left; it pounds like a heart . . .
Surely a dream, but no — she stops and listens
In the ill-lit room; then, brushing her black hair back,
Paces again. There are suitcases by the door
And these tickets are good for a faraway reckless town.

But rain has opened my eyes; I'm miles from the sea.
The wind, like a disappointed wish, is crying,
Or is that all in my throat? Someone beside me
Is stirring in sleep; her hair spreads light on the pillow
And I remember her name from a long way off —
Partly my own, and partly a word I love.

Another faithless dream and I have had many,
But wakened true, though the wind is not forgiving
And the rain drops a bitter message down from the sea.

COMING OF AGE

(after a poem by Charles D'Orleans)

When I heard the drum,
When I heard it say:
"Young men and women come,
It's time to bring in May,"
I could not lift my head;
My pillow, warm and wise,
Soft as a lover, said:
"It is too soon to rise;
Dew has drenched the grass,
Dawn has chilled the air,
Regardless, drummers pass;
You must learn not to care."
When I heard the drum,
When I heard it call:
"Young men and women come,"
I turned and faced the wall.

Green from the apple orchard farther west,
The wind shouldered the grass until it seemed
A tide mounting the hill where we two sat,
And April, you said, was just about to crest.

It was like seeing from its central throne
A realm so total there was ample room
For kindness like yours to counterpoise the hawk
Who dropped through blue attention like a stone.

On such good grounds, unscarred by praise or blame,
We rested. That was, of course, before the world
Had slept with winter, learned to count the change,
And got, among the stars, its evil name.

This speech is toward that girl, but given always
Just too late. Say that I saw her walking
Out of elms, one hand lightly upraised
As to a friend beyond my seeing. Say
She was light against the pillared dusk of boles,
Say it was ankle deep in shade and fall.

I write this on a leaf and send it out
By wind, and if wind drops it at her feet,
And if she doesn't stop to read, or can't,
That's how she is, illiterate as leaves.
I write this because the leaves should know themselves
Just how it is. Expect nothing but praise.

I've done a stupid thing.
Someone is crying because —
I've done this stupid thing.
The world has one more grief.

Let them open their Freud,
Or pray at the church of their choice,
Or track a rat through its maze
To run me a better life.

But I will repeat myself —
Stupid, stupid, stupid,
Repeat and repeat and repeat
On a couple of blind left feet.

This is how, Nathan, you are,
And don't you ever forget —
How you were, and are, and will be,
And worse, what you wanted to be.

If love has one decent word
For even the stupidest man,
Love is the stupidest thing
And suffers what nothing else can.

BLADDER SONG

On a piece of toilet paper
Afloat in unflushed piss,
The fully printed lips of a woman.

Nathan, cheer up! The sewer
Sends you a big red kiss.
Ah, nothing's wasted, if it's human.

When I was sorry for those northernmost people
Whose last winter was absolute, my thought
Of them became a fragile figure asking,
Mostly with starved eyes, could something more
Have been done perhaps, could sorriness have become
An angel, saving more than I ever imagined?
Our planes lifted heavily up through the thin snow
With all that was needed, and yet I stood there wondering
What was left out.

           It was the same again
Far south that earthquake-flood-eruption day
When ceilings and floors all met in one wide shock
And the picture we got was our own disbelief in black
And white; again our planes loaded the basic goods
And went down into the smoke and crying. And again,
That figure arrived — this time with numbed eyes — to ask
What happened to the angel anciently promised for such
Extreme occasions. The planes were burdened with mercy
And the experts for it. What else was there to do?

Angels were made for praising God, His works;
My pity's a partial thing, just like my praise
For human skill, beauty, or justice; and yet
That creature (why do I want to say "child" and why
"Girl child"?) keeps asking long after the event,
As if I had a hand in disaster, could justify
The very worst by parachuting angels down
To show even that worst was only a part
Of some Total, worth her delicate little praise.

What is most hard is that she's beautiful,
As if hunger, disease, and dazed faith create
Their own kind of angel as comfort for those most guilty
Of being far away and helpless. And yet, so pure
Is her asking, that all she seems to need is one man
Who can somehow admit her as real. I try and try,
As she stands here still, like the work of some unknown master,
Full of her miracle and doomed to fly.

The trees won't talk; but we've got instruments
To get the truth. Old omens of the air
Mean birds are hungry, here as everywhere,
And speak, if forced to, in the present tense.
This took eternity and some expense
To verify. Gods, never really there,
Reduce to heroes dying for a share
In prospects disconnected and immense.

Symbols, like homespun drugs, were handy things,
But facts are good as guns. And then there's you —
No priestess circled by sacramental wings
From Cythera, but a girl well suited to the act;
And what's to be done with nature? Nothing new.
We'll dream in symbols, wake up cold in fact.

The messengers kept stumbling in, breathless and bloodshot,
Saying there were risings everywhere else; it was war
And a war of men whose banners scrawled suddenly out:
"Love is not good enough!" though we had sent them bread,
Money, freedom, reasons. We calmed the messengers,
Saw that they tasted fair wine and got a clean bed.

Later, it thundered beyond the hills and the sky
Went stiff, then slowly relaxed; and some of us swore
To vote in the next election, some to send
More charity to our favorite shame, and some,
Sipping choice wine from a fragile silence, computed
The cost of flight toward another kingdom come.

But someone, shadowed by a dusk of leaves,
Kept asking: "Who dreamed you, so improbable
That you are a future nobody even needed?"
He was some Greek or Jew, perhaps, who came
To see his children's children, how they escaped
His law, his love, his unpronounceable name.

This was a pretty country; the vines were new;
The fresh white barn glittered the long noon;
No one had died in the house, no one been born,
Or lived there alone.

Only the oaks, lining the road to the highway,
Hinted of things that maybe happened before,
But their docile shades were dumb, and the lines on their trunks
Spelled "weather," no more.

Then, in the worst fog ever known in that valley,
Something wailed in the cold all night. Was it pain
Or love? Whatever it was, it would surely be mixed
In next year's wine.

Vine leaves grew shaggier — or was it just the eye,
Narrowed by morning wind from the wet hill?
Oaks shivered. And he who leapt out of sleep all hackles
Felt change like a chill.

Just past midnight on the lawn and a thin moon:
Those white tossings may be the flutter of dresses;
They may be petals, for the wind bears in it a sweetness;
And dark dresses there have blended into the lawn.

The musicians, by now far away, doze on their cases;
A spaniel bounds in his sleep toward the ghost of a scent,
And one upper window in all that great house is lighted,
As if someone standing remotely above appraises

The drift of dancers who fell at the very last note
Of the final song that became the wind on their dream.
Fallen as petals, they lie there much at a loss
How ever to keep their vows when the light goes out.

These trees are black. That might be sinister,
And is if it's the kingdom where the trees
Are never black except as omens of
Those gods that only sudden reversals please.
But in a kingdom of transition, note,
The trees shade slow from green to softer dark,
So dusk is sunlight easing down the west
And leaves hide children, making there a park
From which you come much saddened, true, but not
Some traveler in realms of sudden plague
Where everyday's the last and every act,
And what comes after, marvelous and vague.

Which kingdom are these black trees in? The speed
Of darkness varies where we stand to light;
I can remember summer suns so slow
Branches caught fire, burnt far into the night,
Though these on winter's hill are dark and spread
Contagiously. Gone down, even the sun
Seems one more victim. I've heard that other lands
Have clearer signs to read; still others, none.

There is a wall that runs right through the summer,
An adobe wall since summer is Mexico,
And in the shade of the wall the noon is rich.

As rich as sleep, as rich as time, as men
Who rest in it awhile and hear far bells
Upholding heaven with their high-born tongues,

Or, in a fluent native, jacarandas
Lisping minor instances of good,
Of good just now, of lowly nearby good,

Of one adobe summer stretching on
To where the bells are jacarandas shading
Wealthy noon forever in that land

Whose names for things are right, whose time, asleep,
Dreams of the risen poor astride the sun
On one long progress toward the walls of heaven

Which is Mexico and runs through death, right through.

He is leading his grandfather under the sun to market.
Who needs to see? The hand is warm on his shoulder.
The sun tells a man whatever he has to know
And the eyes of the children take care of the rest .

This is a little procession, solemn and steady,
A way of seeing that has the right direction,
And needs the simplest of eyes; the hand is quite sure,
And the wealth of the sun takes care of the rest.

His children have children to spare for any errand
An old man must go on; like sun, they are warmly with him,
Though at night his wakeful hand may remember that seeing
Was going alone in any direction.

Time takes care of the rest. In the niño's eyes
He is leading his grandfather under the sun to market.
In the old man's mind he walks through warmth where he must.
They are going in one direction, and know it.

You hung those bells, señor, to tell you when
And where, but listen how they ring through me.
Like far-off fluttering grief, not yours and not
Quite grief, verdad? I add a little sigh
And, maravilla, everything is changed,
An unintended poignancy blows through,
Making the noon less clear, the walls of night
More night. You call that cloudy music yours?

There is another world, señor, a whole
Harmonious world, but you, though wandering
Ten thousand years, will never enter it
Alive; oh yes, in dreams you see bronze birds
Singing in glades of verdigris, and glimpse
A pale girl beckoning, then, fevered, wake
To hear a fade of garbled bells that mean
A different, different thing, a foreign dawn.

Even these autumn leaves are instances,
Like bells, like songs, like voices once well known;
When heard through me, they translate just beyond
Your latest metaphrase for my most faint
And otherworldly sounds — like far-off bells,
One of my many tongues; yet none is yours,
Señor, but yours are mine, though you at last
Are heard, coughing a little through a wall.

Vatsyayan says, in clearer English than mine,
It is worth having lived, if only to die in the presence
Of a good man, even if — sick — you presume,
On the strength of compassion, the stranger is somehow good.

Then there is God, another presumption perhaps,
But so remote, it always comes back to people:
This shock-eyed girl that no one sees on the bridge,
Or that widower holding twelve pills in his unfelt palm.

One ant, stepped on, of course is unpardonably lost,
Though who can care less — pity's so private, attention
So tender there's only hail and farewell to spare
For the nearest invalid friend. It gets us in dreams.

It is this insoluble self to be any man,
East or west, and to presume on long-lost brothers,
As I presume now on the goodness of Vatsyayan,
And he on the barest hope to be good for others.

Any contract, tax form, Great Idea,
Existentialist brick wall,
Or even the cloudless air provides
Some saving orifice after all,
Through which, well greased, the lawyer, the statesman,
Or the fattest theologian can squeeze,
As can the executive and editor,
And with an almost obscene ease.
The motto over the loophole reads:
"Courage! The end wipes out all means."
God went through two centuries back,
His logic chopped by strict machines.
Peer through: theatres, suburbs, parks,
Factories, monuments, great stores,
A traffic problem. Which is which?
But you're on the proper side, of course.
Some have heard voices from that world —
Distorted, wishful, uttering facts
Terrible in their lack of portent:
Anyone's name (say, John) or acts,
Like loving when it seems to open
The ivory gates for you alone,
But closes, after sex is finished,
On something as alien as stone.

And beware mirrors, not that they open
To evil, but that they can show a face
That seems to look from the other side
Which couldn't be (could it?) so bad a place.

A weather of crows and kites,
The mailman left no mail,
My head is stunned by the sky,
And where will I get a style?

That one has lent me this,
This one has lent me that,
The head that aches is my own
But I've filched this flop of a hat.

These kites are birds, not toys,
Their beaks are hooked to rip,
Maybe a pen should be hooked,
But love has a blunting lip.

The crow comes walloping down,
He has snatched a — what from that pile?
My head is full of the weather
And the weather has no style.

Or is war the minimal style?
A Hell of a note to whistle,
But the crow invaded at dawn,
And the kite angles in like a missile.

And whose is that figure blazoned against the black,
The black you discovered beyond the lights of this city,
Beyond the idea of those lights, beyond that beyond
To the very back of the thought at the very back
Of your thinking? No star is that urgent, no ghost of a god
That intense. These shone for you like a luminous drift
On the midnight pool of your musings when lawns were black,
Great houses black upon black. But this is a blazon,
Figured to be a message against the night
And nearer perhaps than its smallness cries. You must think.

What of the hero? He steps from his story, amazed
That his senseless choice has contained him in outlines of fire,
That his ruin glows of itself for centuries around.
Or the martyr relieved that the blackened torch of his life
Should faithfully burn worlds off through backsliding time.
Or simply a man of troubles who stands them, abashed
That his minimal fire blazes for others to stand by.

But what of the figure out there? You may be dreaming
Again: one flare perhaps only hunting its home,
The merest scruple of light, and it's making the black
More black by its blaze. But it may be the one real thing
In the thought of cities of light in the dark of your time.

AN ANSWER OF SORTS

(to Louis Simpson)

> Born to the suburbs,
> Born to this wasteful middleclass life,
> A neighbor sings in her small backyard,
>
> As if she were in a procession
> To the temple. She has simply forgotten herself
> In the roses. Let her be. Let her be.

It was as though it had begun to rain lightly
On the amazed stillness of birds
And leave-taking was another,
Sadder version of dusk we were attending,
And as though a whole age were going out,
Its head covered, and going out with it
A purpose including stars and stones.

What were their last words
Before the gates shut and small lights
Moved slowly up the hill of dark?

We were to mean everything this once,
Include in what we meant the birds and stars,
The stones too, and be no more watchers
On far shores, on single peaks, listeners
In little rooms, for news of how it is;
We were to hear the true last names for things,
The utter ode, composing us at last
In the rounding music of our sphere.

The gates are shut, the lights over the hill;
The barest voice softens in rain,
Streams out in wind, alleges more in dark than it knows.

Their words are hard to say, hard
To remember when you wake at dawn,
The bare light alerting you to plainness,
Solitude of stones, terror in birds,
Stars drifting off, the feel of huge leave-takings

For which no name, the first or last, consoles.
How can you trust those hints at dusk
Of foreign magnificence?

It may have all begun with a few native words,
Good, but made grandiose by wind or sad by rain,
Our own weather, sparing us a vaster silence.

This is when I turn, trusting you're here,
To say barely what's left, a few last words,
As though leave-taking itself composed
A plain majesty — the way light moved
So slowly up the hill of dark, who held
The light, his special purpose, the grief of gates,
What can't be said, but must. This is to leave
Almost without words, as though dumbfounding
The perfect speakers by including them also
In a fitting goodby.

And this is how stones are spoken for down here,
How birds, how stars, and the foreign mutterings
Of weather, and how men, and what they might mean.

If you're politic over the pool, I will swim
In your net; if you're sly in the woods, I will run
At the bullet you aim; or reward your stealth
In the sky by taking your shot under wing;
If you're quick in the room, I will instantly fall
Whenever you strike; and I will do more:
I will give you this warning — be ready for less
Than you hoped, for less than the trout you netted,
The deer or dove you brought down, the friend
You just floored; for the meat of a shadow is not
The meat of its maker who, now far away,
Looks back at your lessening figure with pity,
But must leave you amazed at your sorry game;
He has other affairs, has other shapes
To try out before dark, and shadows to spare.

If you turn east, slowly, at dawn or dusk,
You see it as a landfall built — look, there! —
Of light; that burnish fired by rising sun,
Or glint looming through gray is Outremer.

You've heard the worst: the perfect Red Cross Knight
Haggling with Syrians over stolen goods,
While wrathful Jews plotted another Zion
By vacant tomb, in the silence of the woods.

But just beyond the desert cities, east,
Just at the end of dark or light, it lies
For those who remember how things should have been:
White houses, sweet-water wells, and vintage skies.

West is another thing — the sails shoulder
Toward golden death and the Hesperides;
But it is back and back to Outremer
And God's own childhood at the Mother's knees.

Let heroes squint through glass for Ind, or snuff
Like dogs at intimations of the clove,
Till, maddened in the crow's nest, they must howl.
We know another, more pacific cove.

In simple linen, pilgrim, come; a sack
For dates, a waterskin, no coin or knife,
Hardly a thought. In Outremer that child
Still waits who has not heard of death, or life.

"Tend to the little things," stone said, "like me
That gives you back your stare until,
Full of each other's look, we'll understand.
I have a door which opens when
Faith makes a seer of your blind right hand."

I went inside that door, and — the whole world
Exactly fitting in one palm —
I held it up. For all the gods strolled here,
Pausing with sovereign concern
To feed and stroke attentive birds or deer.

"Enlil," I called, "Osiris, Yahweh, you;
Odin, Vishnu, and you, Christ,
What are you doing here? Back where I came from
People wonder, shrug, won't wait,
Measuring the moon for Kingdom Come!"

They, infinitely sorry, pointed to my hand
Which only gripped a little stone,
One of ten usual billion. Letting it fall,
I turned. O great catastrophe,
To be so hard, so barren, and so small!

Out here again in this great world I go,
Walking the absence of the gods,
Whose deer leap from my touch, whose birds all wheel
Up crying if I suddenly stir,
Whose sullen stone, cast down, bruises my heel.

On the disintegrated west side of town
A Negro eating supper feels a music;
His fork begins to hum a bitter tune.

The President has set his own fork down
And stares at it. Both diners just this day
Have voted for a man to reach the moon.

Where is that music from? At home in jail,
An inmate raps his knuckles on a bar —
Pain is a furious way of being real.

An old woman is barely paid to wail
A stranger's dying distantly away;
How could her grief get into stainless steel?

And is this the special music of our sphere
That he who listens from the moon will hear?
And is this why we train him not to feel?

And when you come to that hill, the message of summer
Is sunlight riding the crest where the hushing oak
Seems a priesthood of leaves that hymn an indulgent sky;
Now the bear and the snake will recall you again as a brother.
And when she comes out of the shadow under the hill,
The tall grass leans, the little creek alters its course.
The wind comes round, just to be nearer to her,
And the sparrows circle ready to do her will.
That ultimate summer, time fades back like smoke
Miles off, and all broken faiths are mended the instant
You kneel. Not a thing out of place, not the least little stone;
And all is scripture, all is saved by the oak,
And you'll rise from her shade as simple as bear and snake
Whose trails at last lead into the green end of vision
Where all grows together and nothing remains of him
Whose name you have used, who must die for your merciless sake.

This is that other place, north of the last
And most daring flight. Here, driven off course, small birds
Compulsively circle until they drop; the trees
Have marched against it, but always come reeling back.
No leaves, no song. Here, sun and moon are one:
A blinding wheel of snow or sometimes a shine
So pale it would ice the heart if the heart could feel it,
Could come to the middle of white within white and feel.

He, though, has been here, if only in wintering sleep,
Found himself present and breathed in that rigid air
Of no leaves, no song. Thus birds may now live here, and trees,
Though frail, bear the wind. And so we have peopled the place
With the ghost of a snow goose, the hint of a crippled pine,
Merely perhaps to say that here one man
Has stood for the rest of us once to discover that nothing
Is just what we thought without us. And this is his mark.

Ready or not, we are natives now. Though it's cold,
Though the wind refuses our gifts, we know how to praise it.

TRANSLATING AN ANCIENT FRAGMENT

(for Roy Bundy)

A slender skiff runs toward the far shore,
Where, pacing up and down, the Beautiful
Cocks her head to catch the lyric oar.
Thin moon, black water knocking, the white cry of a gull . . .

Men speak brokenly of what most they desire:
Moonlight splinters the bow, the oars dissolve,
The hands open to water, the little fire
Blackens the beach — so much for eternal love.

Yet what ever can stop them going to sea,
Who hear the Beautiful still waits — lost daughter
Of Greek night — to be desired, though they
Be tumbled at her feet, driftwood, revised by water.

There are men who, for no very large
sum, are ready to bring you out of
prison to safety.
> — Crito to Socrates

This is to remember those gunmen of noble causes,
Hired, but not used, waiting with subtle attention
Contracted to another job beyond their ends.

Say three by a dark wall, listening for hustled footsteps
That would whisper, yes, Socrates is afraid, will fly
This very midnight with the help of your circumspect logic.

But no one came, so they edged off; or those few
Who could well have muscled Jesus out of harm's way,
They too may have shrugged and dissolved into darker doings.

No one recalls them. But the hobnailed trooper who muffled
Off Mussolini is still well thought of, at least
In some towns, got his orders and carried them perfectly out.

Which footsteps at night tell how hard, which mouths how urgent
The name of a man? You never are sure of the dark,
Though you try to be just and say a good thing if you can.

Each man to his own good angel. This,
A final version of himself, at tea
With God, and weightless now for having dropped
Every pathetic human thing, like dung.

And this, a spirit greedy after wholeness:
Life including death, the unseen figured
In the seen, the far-away brought close;
One hand up heaven, the other fondling earth.

Or this, an earthen genius springing grass
Of heartfelt green, or dropping autumn leaves,
Bright as doubloons, on every ticklish hand;
A household god and any place its home.

This one, a slender supernatural girl,
The belle who always beautifully says "No,"
And, winged by that refusal, draws her man
To marvels leagues beyond the wide world's end.

And mine? The moody one, who, as you turn,
Is gone, whose absence, like a message, sighs:
"O, I have been all of these and worse; yourself
Meeting yourself with cold, assessing eyes."

These people discuss spirits as if spirits
Were leaves, or might be. They also hint that leaves
Are something more, maybe: like spirits, leaves.

A winter people, they are abstracted much,
Staring at the fire which, they say, is their guest,
A great prince, the sun, lost in the snow.

About pain they are simple; but all the rest they find
More than it is. They have listened to the wind
So long, everything seems strangely kin.

They are a people whose words, lifted by wind,
Take flight like spirits, a people like us maybe,
But poorer, whose leaves mean everything. And must.

It thought it was ripening to swell
Right out of its shell,
And to shoot high as whatever called it
Called it to swell, split, climb, be.
Who needs vision in the dark of growing?

And ready, it dropped
In a basket, borne to a table,
Selected by fingers, shelled and raised
To a mouth, as to big
Sidewise grinding gates.

Briefly, it saw, between shelling
And grinding, the world
It had ripened for, not the world
It had been ripening for:
The wrong world to swell, split, climb, be in.

This is often the way,
Purpose within purpose growing
To no foreseeable end —
God's way, it bitterly supposed
And accepted, as a hero might
Charging gates he did not care to charge,
Thinking about a different place,
About his own sweet life given,
Above his head, to a great cause
Which to someone even higher seemed no cause
At all, but another thing
That wouldn't be explained till the end,
If then.

When the great aptitudes sit alone at midnight,
Some of them empty every bottle, knock
The windows out, then hurl the astonished lamps
At dark, and burn their books. Next dawn, in shock
Most innocent, they wake, and, squinting round,
Are baffled by their dear book's smouldering spine
And dumb disorder. The desk, legs up, seems dead,
And, wringing the curtains, wind cannot explain.

What terrible thought was here to conjure up
The disbelieving devil whose only diet
Is near success, or did the illiterate heart
Get loose again and, as if to deny it,
Spit on mortality? That heart won't learn
And must be always babied back to sleep;
The bottled spirit that is the old solution
Flows to oblivion and is very deep.

Psychiatrists shrug, plain doctors turn their backs
At all this demolition; children, staring,
Clutch small gifts they see will never do
For one like this, who can't quite get his bearing;
And the dead — who know the truth — have no more time
For pity; self-absorbed, they simply hint
A way to judgment. Morning, like the thought
Of God, breaks splendid and irrelevant.

The day that she put on white for good
An apple blossom fell. The bee,
Destined for it, was never seen
Again. Forget apples and honey.

Pain is a kind of blossom too.
She lines toward it, almost unthinking,
Through the long straight corridors,
Bearing her sweetness in a sting.

When she enters, bends and touches,
Whoever has called her holds his breath.
Sexless winter snows the ceiling;
Forget time, forget even death.

Off duty, naked in the bed,
She hardly feels her man's caress;
The white love she has carried home
Numbs them both with tenderness.

And is the apple blossom a pain
The bee relieves, and is honey
A rich oblivion? She thinks,
Dressing for work, she does it for money.

Remember Ralph who ran so fast and far?
Remember Frank who found the way through dark?
Remember Leo who never missed the mark?
And Nick whose hands could bend an iron bar?

Lieutenant Smith — can't you just see him yet?
Always out front, a natural leader, he.
I followed him with you. Remember me?
I am the one who never could forget.

French girls we swore to marry as a whim
Come floating up to mind; it's age I guess;
And are you others having much success?
The prisoner we shot — remember him?

Not since the Army have I held a gun.
I grow rare roses; that wouldn't interest you,
But men should have some different thing to do.
I'd like to hear what all the rest have done.

Lieutenant, still ahead? Nick, just as strong?
Leo, as steady? Frank, still on the track?
And Ralph, as quick? It's quite some distance back,
And who'd have thought one death could take so long?

I. Man and Wife

It's not admitted, but the thing they did
In spring's tall mustard, shadowed by the hill,
Was never equaled, though themselves they've said
The later mellow labor's better still.

I say it's never so and have the proof,
For they are gentle now and keep good rule
Within their house, who, when they had no roof,
Rose from the dawn like twins, divine and cruel.

II. Trial

They never should have married, but they did
And got for their trouble someone to accuse,
To be accused by, someone to whom they could,
With telling pleasure, break the day's bad news . . .
Yet they outlasted friends who foretold just how
And on what day they'd part, and at what place —
But never did; wherever they chose to go,
They went together, bitter and full of grace,
As if some secret (two alone could share)
Bound them by a higher law, though wrong,
Than love's. Like royalty deposed, they were
Impossible, and in that region strong.

III. Father and Daughter

Little now, she's yours, and though she cries
At anger, her whole small heart consents to be
Your darling beyond her pleasure or her pain.
And it's so simple to be good and wise,
You can't see any end. But, though she's plain,
She'll pity you that loved too easily
What she, dressed like a woman for disguise,
Will carry, secret, through unfriendly rain
To him who waits upon her mystery.

Resolved, gentlemen: nothing is resolved.
The gods, though dead, still bleed, if only in
Live pictures of themselves. Achilles' wrath,
Though tented in a book, strides up and down.
Saint Thomas must, though paradised, repeat
In tongues now paper-thin his *sic et non*.
And Bel Aliez, sweet Bel, so long committed
To unhallowed dirt, loves hotly on
And on beneath the greenwood bough — and all
The mighty folk in Hell or Heaven choose
Again, again, their immortality,
Divine compulsives, ordered like the stars
To show where resolution leads.
                                        Suppose
One man elected, only one, to move
As if the wind were with him, though he moves,
Only when ready, toward a lucid air
Whose very breathing quickens him to move
Again. Move thus as he may, this one
Contrives alone to be the lucid breather,
Free himself, and for the earth alone.

Ah, Desiderius, ladies, there he goes:
The Absolute could never find him home,
Was north when he was south, was just too late
To catch him on his way, and lucky too
For both. He could not stand there; when he moved
It was a motion toward and toward, in time
But never mapped. Well, let him go. He carries
Every question in his bag, two sets
Of gods, and all of last year's roses. Stopped,
He writes at stations calmly everything

To learn, then whistles to himself, or, watching
Children, decides deciding is the death
No one has mastered, either north or south.
And on that firm resolve, catches his train.

When they found him pissing against the midnight wall,
His wet forehead leant to the stone,
One hand on the stone to steady the roll of the world
As he leaked out the wine of his body,
When the flashlights stabbed past poplars and slashed through
   boxwood,
He saw them staring with big yellow lenses
And felt the charge of a furious current
That clamped their free right hands to gun butts,
So he wanted to say how he bore with malice toward none
His own darkness, tipsy out of the hole
In his street, over the golf course, melting
Through fences, gliding the grass of the rich,
To wade the swimming pools, burrow through wine cellars
And twine with the roses, because in this precinct
There was no death to live with, no rats to nurse,
No window picturing a face to smash,
And here the lost golf ball could peaceably rest
On giving green, and tubes could float all night
On the kindly support of a warm surface, and he'd reached
This wall to give back some of his good feeling,
But only mumbled. What could they do but hate it?
And slid in under the arms to hoist his sag
Toward the squad car where they quietly beat him, punishing his
   manhood,
Pounding his thoughtful head, their own heads pounding
At all this unreason in manhood, while the rich slept on
Or drank in their hidden depths, also transmitting
Wine through blood into water that steams as it strikes
Cold stone.

Sam Johnson's Black Dog,
Melancholy, is my dog also.
It feeds on guilt, envy, and love
Of a sort; wherever obscurely I go,

It squats on my foot. Some few are crowned,
Millions die for the great cause
Of hunger. I hunt my indulgent dark
For the god that sent me such a hound:

First Cause of the long leash
Of effects, Code in Adam's gene,
Lord of toilet training, Ghost
Stuck in this unsalvageable machine.

Forgive the poet of the woods whose prize
Was solitude with birds that first seemed glad,
Yet sang indifferently. He wrung their necks
In verse; but then their silence drove him mad.

Forgive the city poet. His award —
He ended as the shadow of his name;
On the reverse side of rejection they found scrawled
This epitaph: "That's all there is to fame."

Forgive the wandering poet, based nowhere,
Honored with ticket stubs; at the last station
The Dark Lady put him on his train,
With a broken pen and a bottle of salvation.

The poet of the proud cold tower forgive;
Wore his contempt for crown, spat on base glory,
Climbed up to his work intact and whole,
But, falling down, broke on the common story.

Forgive them this: they only wanted words
To live forever, nothing more. For us,
In woods, cities, or anywhere between,
Obituaries are anonymous.

And one look from the tower plainly shows
It all belongs to death whose style is prose.

I would write more often and better too
If I had the rich address
And the ear, hidden in deep yellow,
Of a princess. I see her now turning to receive
My message; she had been looking into dusk
And watching small lights bloom one by one
Down on the empty street.

You think of birds hovering when she opens the letter
And of good things unfolding.
She sits now, keeping her eyes
On what I have discovered as the only whole hymn
That never could be sung till she existed,
Her name rendered, like a strand of gold,
Through a hundred lines of praise,

Because spirits are at least credible a step from her,
And silence a sort of speech
Between pure strangers met to hear,
As for the first time, even rocks ache
To tell how near they are to what she means
By stooping to locate the least pebble
In the secrecy of its best place.

It is hard to be supernatural and she can do
No good or evil, but accepts
My offering which is to see herself
Lightly bemused, standing finely against
A hundred kinds of dark, and even she,
In the least moment of doubt, can shade
Into the background. She smiles,

Then folds the letter and, looking up, imagines
A brief answer: "You're right . . .
Maybe," and rises to climb the stairs;
Her silks (joined by the silks of attendants) sound
Like a sea in which the motion is felt of far-
Off royal chants, full-sailed, but slow
Bearing her toward my sleep.

A crash of wings just at the crest of May:
My neck hair hackling and the hill grass tense
In that blue silence, cloudless and immense,
Where god, the distance, called. What could I say?

Noon by noon I practiced longing, till
The world edged up to words and I could phrase
The most illusive shadow into praise
Or send out sparrows singing to my will.

Watch how this line glides smoothly up and hovers.
I whistle and, see, it settles on my wrist —
Too tame maybe, but what a vocalist
For undemanding friends and facile lovers.

But sometimes no, oh no: in its pretty beak
A limp thing like a message, or in its stare
A bloodshot notice — answering no man's prayer —
Of what still waits. Then, I'm too scared to speak.

In that town, the Golden Highway ended
At the newly built El Roy Motel
Where I was lodged for a single night's
Luxurious loneness; early next morning,
On a balcony that oversaw
A swimming pool glossed by a delicate wind,
I mused coldly on that green water
And the locked-up sleepers who later would warm it;
And when, in my used-up room, I repacked
And snapped shut the suitcase, the pool flashed
In my mind like a signal winking through sleep;
Through sleep also the truckers loomed on
Toward their coffee stops, towering by
In their tall cabs, looking down, alone;
And alone I left, but — with the high vigilance
Of truckers — took from sleep its warmth;
From water, its green-wind dawn; from going,
A way to leave without goodby.

THE WESLEYAN POETRY PROGRAM

Distinguished contemporary poetry in cloth and paperback editions

ALAN ANSEN: *Disorderly Houses* (1961)

JOHN ASHBERY: *The Tennis Court Oath* (1962)

ROBERT BAGG: *Madonna of the Cello* (1961)

MICHAEL BENEDIKT: *The Body* (1968)

ROBERT BLY: *Silence in the Snowy Fields* (1962)

GRAY BURR: *A Choice of Attitudes* (1969)

TURNER CASSITY: *Watchboy, What of the Night?* (1966)

TRAM COMBS: *saint thomas. poems.* (1965)

DONALD DAVIE: *Events and Wisdoms* (1965); *New and Selected Poems* (1961)

JAMES DICKEY: *Buckdancer's Choice* (1965) [National Book Award in Poetry, 1966]; *Drowning With Others* (1962); *Helmets* (1964)

DAVID FERRY: *On the Way to the Island* (1960)

ROBERT FRANCIS: *The Orb Weaver* (1960)

JOHN HAINES: *Winter News* (1966)

EDWIN HONIG: *Spring Journal: Poems* (1968)

RICHARD HOWARD: *The Damages* (1967); *Quantities* (1962)

BARBARA HOWES: *Light and Dark* (1959)

DAVID IGNATOW: *Figures of the Human* (1964); *Rescue the Dead* (1968); *Say Pardon* (1961)

DONALD JUSTICE: *Night Light* (1967); *The Summer Anniversaries* (1960) [A Lamont Poetry Selection]

CHESTER KALLMAN: *Absent and Present* (1963)

PHILIP LEVINE: *Not This Pig* (1968)

LOU LIPSITZ: *Cold Water* (1967)

JOSEPHINE MILES: *Kinds of Affection* (1967)

VASSAR MILLER: *My Bones Being Wiser* (1963); *Onions and Roses* (1968); *Wage War on Silence* (1960)

W. R. MOSES: *Identities* (1965)

LEONARD NATHAN: *The Day the Perfect Speakers Left* (1969)

DONALD PETERSEN: *The Spectral Boy* (1964)

MARGE PIERCY: *Breaking Camp* (1968)

HYAM PLUTZIK: *Apples from Shinar* (1959)

VERN RUTSALA: *The Window* (1964)

HARVEY SHAPIRO: *Battle Report* (1966)

JON SILKIN: *Poems New and Selected* (1966)

LOUIS SIMPSON: *At the End of the Open Road* (1963) [Pulitzer Prize in Poetry, 1964]; *A Dream of Governors* (1959)

JAMES WRIGHT: *The Branch Will Not Break* (1963); *Saint Judas* (1959); *Shall We Gather at the River* (1968)